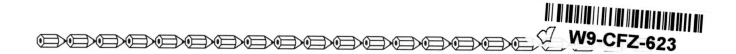

Journal Writing
Activities
for the primary grades

by
Janie Schmidt & Kathy Zaun

Cover Illustration by
Margo de Paulis

Bulletin Board Illustrations by
Julie F. Anderson

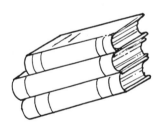

Illustrations of the Creative Writing Pages by
Carol Tiernon

Publishers
Instructional Fair • TS Denison
Grand Rapids, Michigan 49544

Copyright Notice
Instructional Fair • TS Denison grants the right to the individual purchaser to reproduce patterns and student activity materials in this book for noncommercial individual or classroom use only. Reproduction for an entire school or school system is strictly prohibited. No other part of this publication may be reproduced in whole or in part. No part of this publication may be reproduced for storage in a retrieval system, or transmitted in any form or by any means, electronic, mechanical, recording, or otherwise, without the prior written permission of the publisher. For information regarding permission write to: Instructional Fair • TS Denison, P.O. Box 1650, Grand Rapids, MI 49501.

Credits
Project Director: Sherrill B. Flora
Editor: David Carey
Authors: Janie Schmidt & Kathy Zaun
Cover Illustration: Margo de Paulis
Illustrations of Creative Writing Pages: Carol Tiernon
Bulletin Board Illustrations: Julie F. Anderson
Graphic Designer: Deborah Hanson McNiff

Standard Book Number: 1-56822-282-3
Journal Writing Activities for the Primary Grades
Copyright © 1996 by Instructional Fair • TS Denison
2400 Turner Avenue NW
Grand Rapids, Michigan 49544

Introduction

Journal Writing can be a lot of fun for students and the benefits are wonderful! This book is designed to help students enjoy writing and to provide teachers with an endless supply of exciting and educational writing activities.

Journal Writing for the Primary Grades has been organized in twelve sections, divided by months. Important and interesting events which occur each month have been selected as topics for the writing activities. These topics were then categorized into one of the following curriculum areas:

- Language arts
- Social Studies
- Geography
- Science
- Math
- and a monthly Bulletin Board/Learning Center idea

A variety of skills, encompassing everything from drawing pictures, finishing sentences, writing poems, writing homophones, and creating stories to cutting out news articles have been included. As you look through the many topics and activities presented, you will find that the majority of them can be modified to meet the needs and ability levels of your students.

Also included in each of the twelve sections is a Creative Writing Paper featuring many of the events that occur that particular month. This paper is ideal for many of the activities presented and will undoubtedly spark many of your own creative ideas. Simply make copies of the paper for your students and watch them go to work!

Many hours of creative writing fun are found within the pages of *Journal Writing Activities for the Primary Grades.*

Contents

September

September is the ninth month of the year. Its name comes from the Latin word *septem,* which means seven. September was once the seventh month.

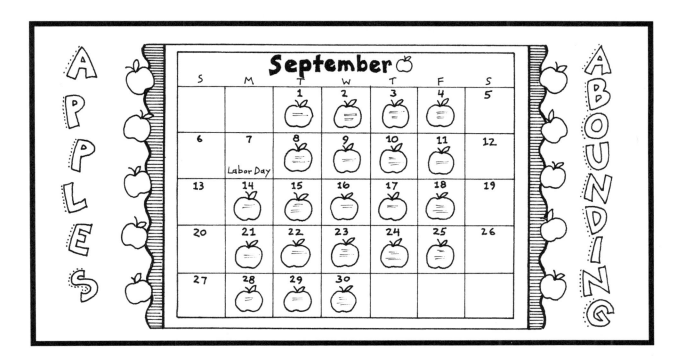

Bulletin Board Idea — Apples Abounding

Make a large calendar or attach one to the center of the bulletin board. Provide the students with red or green construction paper and scissors. The students will make apples that will fit into the daily sections on the calendar. Write a journal activity using the ideas presented in this book, or some of your own ideas, on each of the apples. Attach one for each school day. The students can use the bulletin board to select a writing activity.

Learning Center Idea

Since September is Library Card Sign-Up Month, leave blank cards for the children to practice printing their names and room numbers.

You can also place a large number of library books at the learning center and provide the children with a multitude of activities that center around the library: choose a book to read to a friend, retell a story, draw their favorite character, or write a new ending. There are an infinite number of ideas that can be implemented at a Library Book Learning Center.

September Language Arts

Library Card Sign-Up Month
Library Card Sign-up Month is sponsored by the National Library Association. It is a national effort to sign up every child for a library card.
1. Write a rule about caring for a library book.
2. Read a book. Write the title and the author's name in your journal.
3. Draw an illustration to go with the following title: *Aliens Invade Our School.*

Peter Rabbit's Birthday
In 1893, Beatrix Potter wrote a letter/story to a friend's invalid son about a rabbit and a man who had a garden. The letter later became known as the book, *Tale of Peter Rabbit.*
1. Draw a picture of Peter Rabbit.
2. Name three vegetables that you would plant in a garden.
3. Write a new adventure for Peter Rabbit.

International Literacy Day
September 8th is a special day to promote the importance of being literate.
1. Look up three words in a dictionary and write them in your journal.
2. Cut out an article from a newspaper. Circle all the words that start with the first letter of your name. Older children can circle all the compound words.
3. Write an acrostic poem using the word READ.

First Cartoon Strip
On September 11, 1875, the first cartoon strip "Professor Tigwissel's Burglar Alarm" appeared.
1. Cut a newspaper cartoon strip into sections. Sequence it again.
2. Make up a name for a new comic strip.
3. Make up your own comic strip. Use at least two characters.
4. Write new dialogue for the characters on an existing comic strip.

Jim Henson's Birthday
Jim Henson was a puppeteer born in Greensville, Mississippi on September 24, 1936. He was famous for creating the Muppets. The best known characters are Kermit the Frog, Miss Piggy, Oscar the Grouch and Cookie Monster.
1. Draw a picture of your favorite Muppet. Why do you like this character?
2. Create your own Muppet and give it a name.
3. Write the lyrics to your own Muppet song.

National Farm Animals Awareness Week
The third full week of September is dedicated to promoting awareness of farm animals' natural behaviors.
1. Make a list of parent and baby farm animals.
2. Write about a farm animal that you would like for a pet.

September Social Studies

National Courtesy Month

September is National Courtesy Month. Its purpose is to encourage people to be nice to one another.
1. Write something nice about someone you know.
2. Design a poster for National Courtesy Month.
3. Write three courtesy words.

Labor Day

The first Monday of September is a holiday honoring working people. In 1894, President Grover Cleveland signed a bill making Labor Day an official holiday.
1. Make a list of various careers.
2. Draw a picture of your mom or dad at her/his place of employment.
3. Write a poem about someone who works at your school.

Grandparents Day

Grandparents Day was first proclaimed on September 6, 1979. It is celebrated the first Sunday after Labor Day.
1. Design a special card for your grandparents or for a special older friend.
2. Write three ways that grandparents are special.
3. Draw a picture of what you think you will look like when you are a grandparent.

Citizenship Day

Citizenship Day is on the anniversary of the day the Constitution was approved. It is celebrated September 17 during Constitution Week.
1. Count the number of vowels and consonants in the word citizenship and add them together.
2. Finish the sentence: Being a good citizen means . . . .
3. Make a word search using the word "citizenship."

Emma M. Nutt Day

Emma M. Nutt was the first woman telephone operator in the United States. She began on September 1, 1878, in Boston and worked for thirty-three years.
1. Write your telephone number and address.
2. Write as many words as you can using the word "telephone."
3. Write a list of words that rhyme with call.

Newspaper Carrier Day

A 10 year-old boy named Barney Flaherty became the first "newsboy" in 1833. It was said that he answered an ad in *The New York Sun.* In his honor, September 4 is celebrated as Newspaper Carrier Day.
1. Use an old newspaper and make a collage.
2. Write a story reporting the news.

September Math

National Honey Month

About 230 million pounds of honey are produced each year in the United States.
1. Bees store honey in a six-sided shape. Draw a picture of a six-sided shape.
2. In ancient times, a jar of honey was a sign of wealth. Draw a picture of things that are signs of wealth today.
3. Florida produces 20,900,000 pounds of honey each year. California produces 20,160,000 pounds. Which state produces more?

National Dog Week

The dog has lived with people as a pet for more than 10,000 years. This is longer than any other animal. National Dog Week is celebrated the last full week in September.
1. It is said that each dog year is equal to seven people years. If a dog is 2 in dog years, how old is he in people years. Design your own math problems.
2. Make a chart of the different dogs living with students in your class.
3. Write your own math word problem about dogs.

Swap Ideas Day

Swap Ideas Day is celebrated on the 10th of September.
1. Draw a picture that represents 2+5=7. Swap it with a neighbor.
2. Write a math word problem and swap it with a friend.

Our Capitol's Birthday

The Capitol is the building where the Congress meets. On September 18, 1793, George Washington laid the cornerstone for the Capitol.
1. The Capitol has 540 rooms. Break this number down into hundreds, tens, and ones.
2. Subtract 1793 from this year to see how old the cornerstone is.
3. Draw a diagram of your house or apartment.

National Play-Doh Day

On September 16, 1955, *Play-Doh* was first introduced. Make some of your own: Mix 1 1/2 cups flour, 1/2 cup water, 1/2 cup salt, and 1/4 cup vegetable oil.
1. Name three shapes that you can create with *Play-Doh.*
2. It takes 1 1/2 cups of flour to make *Play-Doh.* How many ounces is that?

Ice Cream Cone's Birthday

The first ice cream cone was invented on September 22, 1903 at the World's Fair in St. Louis.
1. Draw an ice cream cone with four scoops. Number them by tens.
2. What shape is a cone?
3. Some people order single, double, or triple size cones. How many scoops go on each?

September Geography & Science

National Rice Month

Rice is one of the world's most important food crops. More than half the people in the world eat rice as a main part of their diet.

1. Most of the world's rice comes from China. Draw a picture of the country of China.
2. Arkansas is the leading rice state in the United States. Look at the word "Arkansas." Can you see the name of another state?
3. Name two states that border Kansas.

Mayflower Day

On September 16, 1620 the Pilgrims sailed from Plymouth, England on a ship called the *Mayflower.*

1. Draw a picture of the *Mayflower* sailing to America.
2. What ocean did the *Mayflower* cross.
3. Write a story entitled, "When the Pilgrims landed in American they found...."

National Chicken Month

September 9th is the birthday of Colonel Sander's, founder of Kentucky Fried Chicken.

1. Draw a picture of a chicken. Label its comb and wattle.
2. Poultry is included in one of the six food groups in the food pyramid. Name the other groups in the pyramid.
3. Write a chicken recipe.

National Do-It-Yourself Week

National Do-It-Yourself Week is celebrated the 1st week of September. Its purpose is to encourage people to fix things themselves.

1. Draw a picture of something you can do all by yourself.
2. If you could make your own lunch, what would you put in it?
3. Write the directions for how to make a sandwich.

Autumn Begins

Autumn usually begins either September 22 or 23. On the first day of autumn, the sun rises due east and sets due west, which causes an equal amount of light and darkness in a day.

1. Draw a beautiful autumn tree.
2. Make a list of the autumn colors.

National Good Neighbor Day

This event is celebrated on the 4th Sunday in September. This day encourages people to reach out to others in the neighborhood.

1. Draw a map from your house to school.
2. Write two ways that you can be a good neighbor.

September Creative Writing Paper

October

October is the tenth month of the year. Its name comes from the Latin word for eight.

Bulletin Board Idea — Pumpkin Pride

Cover the bulletin board with green paper. Let each student make a small pumpkin using orange and brown construction paper. Attach each of the pumpkins to the pumpkin patch. Write in each of the pumpkins a journal writing activity.

Learning Center Idea

Since October is National Clock Month, you can place all kinds of clocks and watches in the learning center. Let the students work with partners and take turns showing each other various times on the clocks and watches. You can also leave activity sheets in the learning center that show clock faces with various times listed on them. The students can match the times using the real clocks.

October Language Arts

Charlie Brown and Snoopy's Birthday

The "Peanuts" comic strip was first published on October 2, 1950. It was created by Charles Schulz.
1. Draw a picture of your favorite character in the "Peanuts" comic strip.
2. Write the names of four of the "Peanuts" characters.
3. Write you own "Peanuts" comic strip.

National School Lunch Week

The second full week of October is dedicated to good nutrition and wholesome and economical school lunches.
1. Design your own special lunch box.
2. Plan a healthy menu for a week of school lunches.
3. Write a thank-you note to the school cooks.

World Poetry Day

October 15 is World Poetry Day. It is a day to celebrate poetry by reading and writing poems.
1. Write a rhyming poem. Include the words "cat" and "bat."
2. Read a poem to a friend. Write the title and author.
3. Write a poem about yourself. Illustrate the poem.

National Grouch Day

October 15 is a day to honor a grouch!
1. Oscar the Grouch is a famous grouch. Draw a picture of him in his trash can.
2. Write about a thing that makes you feel grouchy.
3. Write three words that describe a grouch.
4. How would you help someone to not feel so grouchy?

Dictionary Day

Noah Webster was born on October 16, 1758. On this day people are encouraged to use a dictionary.
1. Look up the word "pumpkin" in the dictionary. Write its definition.
2. Words are categorized in alphabetical order. Alphabetize the names of ten of your classmates.
3. Many words have two meanings. Write a word which has two meanings. Write the meanings.

National Business Women's Week

The week beginning on the 3rd Monday in October, recognizes the role of the working woman in American society.
1. Make a list of the jobs of four women that you know.
2. Write a campaign speech for the first woman President.

October Social Studies

Universal Children's Week

During the first seven days of October, information on the needs of children are spread throughout the world.

1. Draw a poster for this day.
2. Draw a picture of a child from a country other than your own.
3. Write down three things that you think all children need.

Fire Prevention Week

National Fire Prevention Week is held during the week including October 8. This week marks the anniversary of the great Chicago fire of 1871.

1. Design a fire safety poster.
2. List five ways to help prevent fires.
3. Write a plan of what to do in your home in case of a fire.

Family History Month

During the month of October, people are encouraged to pass on important family stories, customs, and traditions to their children.

1. Write a funny story that happened to your family.
2. Draw your family tree.
3. Write a family custom that your parents have shared with you.

Energy Awareness Month

During October a greater understanding of energy sources is promoted.

1. Draw or write the names of as many things as you can see right now that use energy.
2. Write a list of words that rhyme with "light."
3. What do you like to do when you have a lot of energy?

P.T. Barnum First Introduced the Circus

"The Greatest Show on Earth" is how P.T. Barnum described his first circus which opened October 20, 1871.

1. Three different circus acts happen at the same time in three different rings. Draw your favorite circus act.
2. Jumbo, the elephant, was made famous by P.T. Barnum. Write some sentences that describe an elephant.
3. Write a list of at least ten words that relate to a circus.

Theodore Roosevelt's Birthday

Theodore Roosevelt, the 26th President of the United States was born on October 27, 1858.

1. "Teddy" was a nickname for Theodore Roosevelt. Design a Teddy bear.
2. Write the names of six different United States Presidents.
3. Find a picture of Theodore Roosevelt. Draw a picture of him.

October Math

National Popcorn Poppin' Month

October is dedicated to the celebration of popcorn as a wholesome, economical and natural food.
1. Write a recipe for a popcorn treat.
2. Make a graph showing how many children in your class like popcorn.
3. Write a math problem using popcorn.

National Clock Month

During this month, people are encouraged to realize the importance clocks play in their lives.
1. Draw three different kinds of clocks, each showing a different time.
2. List what time you go to bed, get up in the morning, go to school, eat lunch, and get home from school.
3. Write a word problem involving time. Give it to a friend to solve.

National Pizza Month

Pizza is often called "America's Number One Fun Food." During National Pizza Month, the nutrition of pizza is promoted.
1. Draw your favorite pizza. Cut it in half, then into fourths, and finally into eighths.
2. Take a poll in your classroom about which company makes the best pizza in your town.

National Metric Week

During the second week of October people are encouraged to become aware of the importance of the metric system.
1. Write how tall you are in meters.
2. Measure something. Write its length in centimeters and inches.
3. A United States dollar weighs about one gram. Write the weight for 3 dollar bills, 5 dollar bills, and 10 dollar bills.

Standard Time Resumes

During the last Sunday in October, most places in the United States set their clocks back one hour, to standard time.
1. Draw a clock face. Write the time one hour later than it really is.
2. Look at a calendar. How many Sundays are in the month of October?

Halloween

October 31 is Halloween, a holiday that is celebrated with trick-or-treating and dressing up in costumes.
1. Draw one pumpkin to represent each year of your life.
2. Draw 5 little ghosts. On each ghost write a math problem and the answer.
3. Draw a big spider with eight legs. Write a math problem on each leg.

October Geography & Science

United Nations Day

United Nations Day is observed October 24. This organization works to promote world peace.
1. Draw a picture of a flag from one of the countries that is a member of the United Nations.
2. Write a poem about peace.
3. Write the names of five countries that are members of the United Nations.

Columbus Day

Columbus Day is observed the second Monday in October. It celebrates the anniversary of Christopher Columbus' arrival on a Caribbean Island on October 12, 1492.
1. Draw a picture of the *Nina, Pinta* and *Santa Maria.*
2. Make a map for Columbus to follow.
3. Make a list of some of the new things that Columbus saw when he landed.

National Seafood Month

This month is dedicated to promoting the taste and variety of seafood.
1. Make a list of four oceans.
2. Make a list of some types of seafood that people eat.
3. Make a poster promoting seafood.

National Dental Hygiene Week

This third week in October was established to help people become aware of the importance of preventive dental health care.
1. List three things that you can do to prevent cavities.
2. Design a poster that teaches children how to properly brush their teeth.

Computer Learning Month

Computer Learning Month promotes the learning of new uses of computers and software.
1. Write five words that relate to a computer.
2. Make as many words as you can from the word "computer."
3. Design a new computer. What does yours look like?

International Space Hall of Fame Induction

Each year on the first Saturday in October, deserving space pioneers and explorers are inducted into the International Space Hall of Fame.
1. Design a spacecraft that you would like to ride in.
2. Write the names of the nine planets.
3. Write the name of a famous astronaut. What did that astronaut do that made him/her famous?

October Creative Writing Paper

CHILDREN'S DAY

FALL BACK

POEMS

POETRY

Dear Juan,
How are you? I am fine. It is fun having a pen pal in Mexico! Please send me a photo of

BIG TOP

November

November is the eleventh month of the year. Its name comes from *novem,* the Latin word for nine. November at one time was the ninth month.

Bulletin Board Idea — Amazing Authors

November is the month that hosts National Children's Book Week and National Author's Day. To celebrate these events let each student decorate a sheet of paper to resemble the cover of their favorite book. Have the students retell the story in their own words and illustrate several of their favorite scenes from the story.

Learning Center Idea

November is Peanut Butter Lover's Month. In a learning center, place as many kinds of peanut butter products as you can find. The students can help with this project by bringing in some items from home. You may want to include other foods that might go well with peanut butter. The students can perform some taste-testing experiments by putting the various foods and peanut butter together.

November Language Arts

National Author's Day

National Author's Day is held on November 1st. This day is celebrated to honor those people who have made important contributions to the world of literature.
1. Draw a picture of what you think your favorite author looks like.
2. Make a list of as many of your favorite authors as possible.
3. If you became an important author, what type of books would you write?

National Children's Book Week

The events during the third week of November are held to encourage children to read for pleasure.
1. Draw a picture and write a sentence about a favorite story book character.
2. Make a list of as many of your favorite stories as possible.
3. Design a new book jacket for one of your favorite stories.

Peanut Butters Lover's Month

November is dedicated to this favorite food and to the sandwich it creates!
1. Make a list of all the peanut butter foods you like.
2. Write a recipe for a food containing peanut butter.
3. Finish this sentence: In my peanut butter sandwich I saw a . . . .

Sandwich Day

November 3 is the birthday of the Earl of Sandwich, John Montague, the inventor of the sandwich.
1. Write a recipe of your favorite sandwich.
2. Make a list of places where you can buy a sandwich.
3. Draw a picture and write a sentence about your favorite sandwich.

1st Black Professional Hockey Player

On November 15, 1950, Arthur Dorrington became the first Black man to play organized hockey in the United States.
1. Write about something that you would like to be the first to do.
2. Make a list of all the things you would need to play hockey.
3. Write a poem about hockey.

Mickey Mouse's Birthday

Mickey Mouse first appeared on November 18, 1928 in a film called *Steamboat Willie.*
1. Draw a picture of Mickey Mouse.
2. Write the names of five of Mickey 's friends.
3. Make a birthday card for Mickey Mouse.
4. Write the names of the states where you could go and see Mickey Mouse.

November Social Studies

Native American Indian Heritage Month
November is a time to celebrate the Native American culture and traditions.
1. Write the names of at least three Native American tribes.
2. Write the name of a famous Native American.
3. Write a description of how the Native Americans helped the first settlers in America.

Latin America Week
Events held during the fourth week of November are designed to promote an understanding of Latin American countries.
1. Write the name of three Latin American countries.
2. Write a letter to someone who lives in a Latin American country. Tell them about your country.
3. Draw a picture of you in Mexico.

Elephant Became Republican Party's Symbol
On November 7, 1874 the elephant first appeared in a political cartoon in a magazine. It remains a symbol of the Republican party.
1. Draw a picture of the symbol of the Democratic party.
2. Draw a new symbol to represent your school.
3. Describe what your school's symbol means.

Election Day
Many state, local, and national government elections are held the first Tuesday after the first Monday in November.
1. Design a campaign button for someone you want to win an election.
2. Write the name of the President of the United States.
3. Why would you make a good president?

American Education Week
The events during this week focus on the importance of education.
1. Who is your favorite teacher? Why?
2. What is your favorite subject in school? Why?
3. Why do you think it is important to get a good education?

Thanksgiving Day
Thanksgiving Day is celebrated on the fourth Thursday in November.
1. Many people eat a large Thanksgiving dinner. Write a list of the food that you eat on Thanksgiving.
2. Write about something for which you are thankful.
3. Draw a turkey using the shape of your hand.
4. Write about the first Thanksgiving.

November Math

Daniel Boone's Birthday
Daniel Boone, the most famous pioneer of colonial times was born on November 2, 1734.
1. Boone died in 1820. How old was he?
2. When Daniel Boone was twelve, he began to hunt. What year was this?
3. How many years ago was Daniel Boone born? How many years ago did he die?

First Professional Football Player
On November 12, 1892, the first professional football player, William "Pudge" Heffelfinger, was paid $25.00 for expenses and a cash bonus of $500.00.
1. How much money does your favorite football player earn a year?
2. Create a math word problem using footballs.
3. Locate some football scores (make them up or find these scores in a newspaper), and write three math problems using these scores.

Around the World in 72 days
On November 14, 1889, Nellie Bly, a newspaper reporter, traveled around the world in 72 days, 6 hours, 11 minutes and 14 seconds.
1. What day will it be in 72 days?
2. How many minutes are in 6 hours?
3. Draw a picture of the vehicle that you would use to travel around the world.

National Community Education Day
This day is held the Tuesday during American Education Week to promote strong relationships between the schools and the communities they serve.
1. How many teachers are there in your school building?
2. Make a chart and graph the favorite subjects of the students in your class.
3. Write the name of your community. How many letters in the name?

National Game & Puzzle Week
The last week of November is dedicated to helping people appreciate games and puzzles as a way to constructively spend time with family and friends.
1. Make up a new number game that you can play with a friend.
2. Color a picture and cut it into puzzle pieces. Give it to a friend to put together again.
3. Make up a word search. Include the names of three friends.

Speed Limit Changed to 55 m.p.h.
On November 25, 1973, the national speed limit was changed from 70 m.p.h. to 55 m.p.h..
1. How many m.p.h. were reduced from 70 m.p.h. to 55 m.p.h.?
2. Write a math problem using speed limits.

November Geography & Science

World Communication Week

The first seven days of November are dedicated to putting great emphasis on the importance of communication among over 5 billion people in the world.
1. Cut out pictures of things which help people communicate.
2. More than 3,000 languages are spoken in the world. Write the names of three of them.
3. Write the name of the country you would most like to visit.

Veterans Day

Veteran's Day honors all men and women who have served in the United States Armed Services.
1. What countries were involved in World War I?
2. Write the name of a war that was fought in the United States.

World "Hello" Day

On November 21, everyone who wants to participate in this event should greet 10 people to promote peace through personal communication.
1. Write the word "hello" in another language.
2. Draw a picture of something you think looks peaceful.
3. Write the name of a country that does not have peace.

Aviation History Month

This month is dedicated to the science of aviation and flight as a result of the aeronautical experiments done by two French brothers in November, 1782. These experiments led to the invention of the hot air balloon.
1. Design a new flying machine.
2. Draw and color a hot air balloon. Why do you think it flies?
3. Write the name of a famous airplane.

United Nations: International Week of Science and Peace

This week is dedicated to activities designed to increase public interest in science and peace and their effect on each other.
1. Write five words relating to peace.
2. Write about a science topic that you would like to learn more about.
3. Make a collage of things that are helpful in society.

Great American Smokeout

The third Thursday in November is dedicated to encouraging smokers to quit smoking for at least 24 hours.
1. Write why smoking is bad for you.
2. Create a poster for this event.
3. Write a letter asking someone you know to quit smoking.

November Creative Writing Paper

December

December is the twelfth and last month of the year. Its name comes from the Latin word *decem,* which means ten.

Bulletin Board Idea — What Great Weather!

Provide the children with a variety of colored construction paper, scissors, glue, and markers. Have the students make pictures or symbols of fun things that they like to do during the month of December. If you live in a cold, snowy climate, the students may create pictures of skating and sledding. Have the children write a short narrative to go with their pictures. Let the children share their pictures with the class before you pin them to the bulletin board.

Learning Center Idea

Bingo was first invented during the month of December. Provide the children with a Bingo learning center. Have a variety of Bingo games available for the students: Color Bingo, Number Bingo, Sight Word Bingo, Picture Bingo, Spelling Word, and blank grids and cards for the children to design their own original Bingo games.

December Language Arts

Walt Disney's Birthday

Walt Disney was born on December 5, 1901. He created the famous cartoon character Mickey Mouse.

1. Draw a picture of Mickey Mouse and then design a new friend for Mickey.
2. Make a list of Mickey's friends.
3. If Walt Disney were still alive, what would you like to ask him?

St. Nicholas' Day

On December 6, one of the most honored saints is recognized.

1. Write about the best present that you ever received.
2. Draw a picture of what you think Saint Nicholas looked like.
3. Make a list of the times when people give presents.

UNICEF established

The United Nations International Children's Emergency Fund was established on December 11, 1946.

1. Write a thank-you letter to someone who has helped a child.
2. Many children collect money for UNICEF. Design a can for collecting money.
3. Draw a picture of a child from another country, dressed in that country's authentic clothing.

Bill of Rights Day

On December 15, 1791, the first 10 amendments, known as the Bill of Rights, were added to the Constitution.

1. Look up the word "amendment" in the dictionary. Write the definition.
2. Write three words that rhyme with "right."

Eat What You Want Day

December 16 is a day set aside for everyone to enjoy eating what they want!

1. Make a list of some of your favorite foods.
2. Write a menu for the day.
3. Make a word search to give to a friend. Include 5 of your favorite foods in the word search.

Tell Someone They're Doing a Good Job Week

During the third week of December, tell someone that they are doing a good job.

1. Write the names of three people you think do a good job.
2. Design an award to give someone who does a good job.
3. Write about something that you do well.
4. Write three words that mean the same as "great." Use a thesaurus.

December Social Studies

Boston Tea Party

On December 16, 1773, Boston patriots dumped about 350 chests of British tea into the Boston Harbor. The colonists did this because they were not pleased about being forced to pay taxes to the British.

1. Why do you think people pay taxes?
2. Draw a picture of you at the Boston Tea Party.
3. Draw a picture of, and label, your favorite beverage.
4. Write a list of words that rhyme with "tea."

Las Posadas

Las Posadas is a Mexican celebration that recreates the journey of Mary and Joseph, as they searched for lodging in Bethlehem before Christ was born. Masses are celebrated outside each night beginning on the 16th of December and continuing for nine days until the 24th.

1. In a procession, led by people dressed as Mary and Joseph, people stop and visit homes along the way. Draw a picture of a Mexican home that you would like to visit.
2. A piñata is a favorite part of the celebration. Design a piñata.
3. Make a list of the things that you would put inside the piñata.

Hanukkah

The Jewish Festival of Lights, is an eight-day celebration that remembers the great miracle when the lamp in the temple, which only had enough oil for one day, kept burning for eight days and nights, giving the Jewish people enough time to prepare more oil.

1. Draw a menorah. It is a special candelabra.
2. Gelt in Yiddish means Hanukkah money (gold coins). Write what you would to with your gelt.
3. Write a list of people to whom you would like to give a present.

Christmas

Christmas celebrates the birth of Jesus Christ. Christmas day is December 25.

1. Draw a picture of a beautifully decorated Christmas tree.
2. Write about your favorite holiday tradition.
3. What are some special things that your family does during the month of December?

Kwanzaa

This African-American family observance began in 1966. In recognition of traditional African harvest festivals, this celebration stresses the unity of family. This seven-day celebration begins December 26 and lasts until January 1.

1. A community-wide harvest feast (karamu) is held on the seventh day. Write a list of the foods you would include.
2. Draw a picture of something that grows in your region.

December Math

Bingo Birthday Month
Edwin S. Lowe developed and manufactured the game of Bingo in 1929. Today it is still a very popular game.
1. Design a new Bingo game.
2. Write the names of as many Bingo games as you can.
3. Write a Bingo game card with math facts.

Melvil Dewey's Birthday
Melvil Dewey, the inventor of the Dewey decimal book classification system, was born on December 10, 1851.
1. Write the 10 categories of the Dewey decimal system.
2. In which category can you find your favorite books?
3. Design a poster encouraging people to read.

Alexandre Gustave Eiffel's Birthday
Alexandre Gustave Eiffel was a French engineer who designed the Eiffel Tower in Paris, France. He was born on December 15, 1832.
1. The Eiffel Tower is 984 feet high. How much taller is the tower than you?
2. It cost over 1 million dollars to build. Write the numeral 1 million.
3. Draw a picture of the Eiffel Tower.

Wright Brothers' First Powered Flight
On December 17, 1903, Orville and Wilbur Wright flew the first powered and controlled airplane.
1. The flight lasted less than one minute. How many seconds are in one minute?
2. How many hours are in a day ?
3. Write a word problem involving time and an airplane.

Metric Conversion Act
This act, passed on December 23, 1975, established that the International System of Units (metric) will be this country's basic system of measurement.
1. Draw a line 6 inches long. How many centimeters is this?
2. Measure your pencil in inches and then in centimeters.
3. How tall are you using the metric system?

Isaac Newton's Birthday
Sir Isaac Newton, a mathematician, scientist and author, was born on December 25, 1642.
1. Write a math word problem involving gears.
2. Make a birthday card for this mathematician.
3. Using the word "Isaac" and the following code, what would be the total?
   I=1, s=2, a=3, c=4 (answer:13)

December Geography & Science

Pearl Harbor Day

On December 7, 1941, about 200 Japanese aircraft attacked Pearl Harbor, Hawaii. About 3,000 people died. This caused the United States to enter World War II.
1. How many islands make up the state of Hawaii?
2. Volcanoes are found in Hawaii. Draw a picture of a volcano.
3. How is the state of Hawaii different from your state?

South Pole Discovered

On December 14, 1911, Roald Amundsen and four companions were the first to visit the South Pole.
1. Write the name of the "other" pole.
2. What are some animals that inhabit the South Pole?
3. The South Pole is part of what continent?

Louisiana Purchase Day

The United States bought the Louisiana Territory from France on December 20, 1803.
1. The land cost about $20.00 a square mile. What are some things that you can do within a mile of your house?
2. Write two words in French.

Poinsettia Day

Dr. Joel Roberts Poinsett introduced the poinsettia plant into the United States. He died on December 12 and is celebrated as Poinsettia Day.
1. Draw a picture of a poinsettia.
2. Make a list of all the things that a plant needs in order to grow.
3. Make a list of your favorite foods that come from plants.

National Flashlight Day

This day occurs on the longest night of the year, the Winter Solstice, when people can use a flashlight the most.
1. Draw a super duper flashlight. Write what it can do.
2. Write examples of when and why people use flashlights.
3. Besides flashlights, draw a picture of other devises used to help people see in the dark.

Winter Begins

On December 21 or 22, winter begins in the northern hemisphere.
1. Write what season it is in the southern hemisphere on those days.
2. Write a poem about winter. What things can you do in winter?
3. Draw a snowflake. How many points does a snowflake have? (answer: 6)

December Creative Writing Paper

January

January is the first month of the year. It is named for Janus, a mythological Roman God.

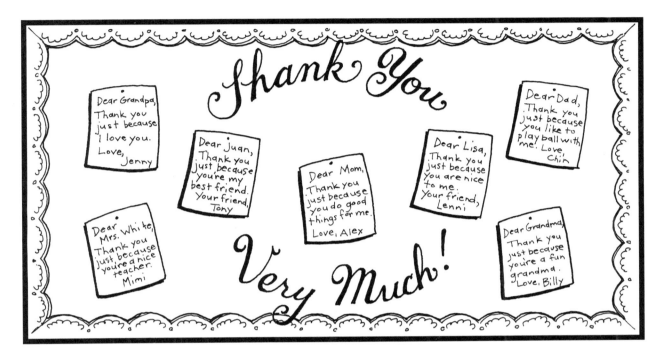

Bulletin Board Idea — Thank You Very Much!

January includes National Thank You Day. To celebrate this day, have each of the students write someone a thank-you note. It's nice to send a person a thank-you for a gift, but we can also send thank-you notes "just because" — just because you were nice to me, just because you are my friend, just because I love you, etc.

Have the children make two copies of their thank-you cards. One copy to be mailed and the other copy for display on the bulletin board.

Learning Center Idea

Inauguration Day is January 20. In a learning center, provide the students with newspapers and magazines containing information about the President of the United States.

Encourage each child to make a campaign poster which nominates that student for president. Have the children write one or two reasons why they would be a good president.

Plan your inauguration celebration. Make a list of who you would invite. Remember that you are the President and that you can invite anyone you wish. Who would you put on your "wish list."

January Language Arts

National Thank You Day

January 11 is a day for you to say "thank you" to someone who has done something nice for you.
1. Write a thank-you letter to someone.
2. Design a thank-you card with a colorful illustration.
3. Write the words "thank-you" in another language.

Pooh Day

A.A. Milne, the author of *Winnie the Pooh* books, was born January 18, 1882.
1. Write a story about you and Winnie the Pooh.
2. Draw a picture of your favorite bear.
3. Finish the sentence: One day, Pooh and I saw. . . .

Inauguration Day

The term of the president of the United States begins on January 20th.
1. An inauguration ball is usually held after the president is sworn in. Draw what you would like to wear to the party.
2. Write what you would do for your country if you were president.
3. Write the name of the president and vice-president of the United States.

National Handwriting Day

This day is held on John Hancock's birthday, January 23, to encourage more legible handwriting.
1. Write the definition of "legible."
2. Practice writing your full name ten times.
3. Write a letter to a friend in your best handwriting.

Mozart Week

One of the world's greatest musicians and composers, Wolfgang Amadeus Mozart was born on January 27, 1756. Mozart Week is celebrated during the week containing Mozart's birthday.
1. Write the name of your favorite musician.
2. Write the name of your favorite song.
3. Draw a picture of yourself playing a musical instrument.

Universal Letter Writing Week

During this week, people should send letters to friends in the United States and in other countries.
1. Write a letter to someone in another country. Tell him/her about your country.
2. Make a card to send someone who lives in another state or province. Tell them something special about your community.
3. Draw a picture of your home. Send it to a friend.

January Social Studies

New Year's Day

New Year's Day, celebrated January 1, is the world's most-widely celebrated holiday.
1. Write a New Year's resolution.
2. List the names of as many holidays as you can.
3. Draw a picture of your favorite holiday.

Betsy Ross's Birthday

Born on January 1, 1752, Betsy Ross is believed to have created the first stars-and-stripes flag.
1. Draw the United States flag.
2. Write why there are 50 stars on the flag.
3. Write why there are 13 stripes on the flag.

Louis Braille's Birthday

Louis Braille, inventor of the touch system of reading and writing for the blind, was born January 4, 1809.
1. If someone who was blind wanted to know what you look like, write down what you would tell that person.
2. Locate a copy of the Braille alphabet. Write your first name using the Braille dots.

Martin Luther King, Jr.'s Birthday

Martin Luther King, Jr., a civil rights leader, minister, and recipient of the Nobel Peace Prize, was born on January 15, 1929.
1. Martin Luther King, Jr., believed in nonviolence. Write what you think "non-violence" means.
2. Design and draw a sign that you could carry in public about the importance of civil rights .
3. Write the names of several other great African-Americans.

John Hancock's Birthday

John Hancock was born on January 23, 1737. He is well-known as the first signer of the Declaration of Independence.
1. Locate where the Declaration of Independence was signed.
2. Make a list of at least eight other people who signed the Declaration of Independence.
3. Write a paragraph about what you think the phrase "Give me your John Hancock" means.

January Math

Everyman's Birthday

January 1 is often called Everyman's Birthday. In some countries, a year is added to everyone's age on this day instead of on their true birthday.

1. How old are you? How old will you be on your next birthday? How old will you be in five years? In ten years? In 20 years?
2. How old would everyone in your house be if today was Everyman's birthday?
3. Create a birthday card. Draw a cake with the number of candles that equal your age.

General Tom Thumb's Birthday

On January 4, 1838, Charles S. Stratton (Tom Thumb) was born. He was one of the world's most famous midgets.

1. Tom Thumb grew to 3 feet 4 inches. How tall are you?
2. Seventy pounds is all that Tom Thumb weighed. How much more or less do you weigh than Tom.
3. Figure how old Tom Thumb would be if he was still living today.

Gold Discovered in California

Gold was accidentally discovered on January 24, 1848 in California. This began the historic "Gold Rush."

1. Describe what you would do if you found a bag of gold.
2. Make a list of some things that are made from gold.
3. Write a math word problem using gold.
4. Write the name of another valuable mineral.

Elementary School Teacher's Day

This special day is celebrated on the third Monday in January, and is dedicated to the professionals who teach children.

1. How many teachers are there at your school?
2. Count how many teachers are female and how many are male. Which group is the largest? Which group is the smallest? What is the difference?
3. Write a math lesson plan for the day.

National Pie Day

National Pie Day is January 23.

1. List and number all of the kinds of pies you can think of.
2. Make a graph showing how many children in your class like apple pie, lemon pie or chocolate pie. Which is the favorite? Which is the least favorite?
3. Write a recipe for your favorite pie.
4. If there are eight pieces of pie and your friends eat half, how many pieces of pie do you have left?

January Geography & Science

Alaska Admission Day

Alaska became the 49th state of the United States of America on January 3, 1959.
1. Write the numeral for the total number of states in the United States of America.
2. Draw a map of your state.
3. Identify the name of the continent on which Alaska is located.

Oil Discovered in Texas

On January 10, 1901, oil was discovered in Texas.
1. Draw a map of the state of Texas.
2. Write about something you might see in Texas that you would not see where you live.
3. Make a list of some of the animals that you could see in Texas.
4. Write about some different uses for oil.

National Hat Day

January 20, is a day when people are encouraged to wear a hat.
1. Draw a picture of a funny hat.
2. Make a collage of people who wear hats at work.
3. Design a state hat for the people of your state.

National Eye Care Month

This month is dedicated to teaching people to seek medical eye care to prevent diseases of the eye or blindness.
1. Draw a picture of your eyes. (Older children may want to label parts of the eye.)
2. Sight is one of the five senses. Write the other four.
3. Write five words that rhyme with eye.

Benjamin Franklin's Birthday

Benjamin Franklin was born on January 17, 1706. He invented bifocal glasses, a lightening rod, the Franklin stove and experimented with electricity.
1. Draw a picture of something you invented.
2. Draw a picture of a light bulb. Label its parts.
3. Write the safety rules about flying kites.

Apollo 14 Landed on the Moon

On January 31, 1971, astronauts Alan B. Shepard, Jr. and Edgar D. Mitchell were launched on a mission to land on the moon.
1. Draw a space craft that you would like to ride in.
2. Write the names of the nine planets.
3. Imagine that were on Apollo 14. Describe your trip.

January Creative Writing Paper

February

February is the second and the shortest month of the year. Its Latin name, *Februarius,* means to purify.

Bulletin Board Idea — What a Great Idea!

This month we celebrate National New Idea Week. Cover the bulletin board with light blue paper. Draw and color a large light bulb in the center of the bulletin board. Each day give the students a new topic to write about. The students must come up with a new idea for that topic. For example, the topic could be "School." A new idea would be to purchase ponies for all the children to ride at recess. Have the children illustrate their new ideas for the bulletin board.

Learning Center Idea

February is National Snack Food Month. Talk about proper nutrition and the importance of eating healthy foods. Snacks can also be healthy and help contribute to a well-balanced meal plan. In the learning center provide the children with many food wrappers , food labels and newspaper and magazine food advertisements. The children can use these materials to help create a healthy food placemat. The students can cut out the pictures and glue them onto an 11" x 17" sheet of construction paper. Laminate for durability. Keep these placemats at school and use them during snacktime or special parties.

February Language Arts

Boost Your Self-Esteem Month

February is dedicated to helping people boost their self-esteem and to encourage people to accept new challenges.

1. Write three ways in which you are helpful to others.
2. Make a card telling a friend that he/she is special.
3. Draw a picture of yourself doing something nice for someone else.
4. Using each letter of your name, write a list of positive words that describe your personality.

National New Idea Week

During the first week of February, people are encouraged to come up with new ideas and to put them into action.

1. Cut out a light bulb and write an idea on it.
2. Draw a picture of an idea that would benefit your whole class.
3. Finish this sentence: The best idea I ever had was . . . .
4. Write about an idea that you have had for a fun family activity.

Valentine's Day

February 14 is a widely observed holiday during which people exchange gifts and cards.

1. Make a Valentine's Day card for a friend.
2. Write a rhyming Valentine message.
3. Draw a large heart. Fill the heart with words that remind you of Valentine's Day.
4. Write about your favorite Valentine's Day.

Student Volunteer Day

February 20 honors students who donate their time to helping others and their communities.

1. Write one way you could help your community.
2. Write the name of a volunteer organization in your community.
3. Design a poster for this day.
4. Finish this sentence: A Volunteer is . . . .

National Pancake Week

National Pancake Week is held the last week of February and its purpose is to recognize the popularity of pancakes.

1. Make a list of all the good things that you can put on a pancake.
2. Write a story about a pancake that rolled off your plate.
3. Make a collage of many good breakfast foods.
4. Write about another food that you think should be honored.

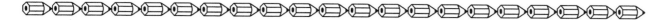

February Social Studies

African-American History Month
February is dedicated to the achievement and contributions made by African-Americans.
1. Make a list of famous African-Americans.
2. Cut out a newspaper article about a famous African-American.
3. Make a collage of famous African-Americans.
4. Write a story about an African-American that you admire.

National Freedom Day
On February 1, 1895, President Abraham Lincoln approved the 13th Amendment to the U.S. Constitution which abolished slavery. This day is celebrated as National Freedom Day.
1. Finish this sentence: Freedom means . . . .
2. Make a collage of all the things that you are free to do.
3. Write about what your life would be like if you were not free.
4. Write five words that rhyme with free.

Boy Scouts of America Week
The Boy Scouts of America Week is held during the week containing February 8, and celebrates the founding of the Boy Scouts.
1. This organization helps to teach young people how to become good citizens. Write about one way in which you are a good citizen.
2. Boy Scouts are trained to become leaders. Write about how you will learn to be a leader.
3. The Boys Scout's motto is "Be Prepared." Explain why it is important to be prepared.

Abraham Lincoln's Birthday
Born February 12, 1809, Lincoln was the 16th president of the United States.
1. Write the name of today's president.
2. Write the names of at least three other presidents.
3. Draw a picture of the White House.
4. Lincoln was born in a log cabin. Write about what you think it would be like to live in a log cabin.

George Washington's Birthday
George Washington, the first president of the United States, was born on February 22, 1732.
1. Draw a picture of the kind of tree that George Washington supposedly cut down when he was a child.
2. Finish this sentence: I would be a great president because. . . .
3. George Washington said that he could not tell a lie. Have you ever told a lie? Write about a lie you might have told.

February Math

Humpback Whale Awareness Month
February is dedicated to educating people about the humpback whale.
1. Humpback whales grow no longer than fifty feet. Draw a humpback whale one foot long.
2. Humpback flippers are about one-third as long as their body. Draw a square and divide it into three equal parts.
3. Measure something that is about fifty feet long. Write the name of this item.
4. Write a story about a pretend ride you took on a whale.

National Pet Owner's Month
During February, people are encouraged to take better care of their pets and appreciate the joy a pet can bring.
1. Find out and graph how many students have a dog, a cat, or both a dog and cat.
2. Write a math problem involving a pet.
3. A bag of dog food holds 8 cups. Your dog eats one-half cup of food a day. In how many days will the bag be empty?

Charles Lindbergh's Birthday
Born on February 4, 1902, Lindbergh was the first to fly solo and nonstop over the Atlantic Ocean.
1. Charles Lindbergh died in 1974. How old was he when he died?
2. Write a math word problem about airplanes.
3. It took Lindbergh $33 1/2$ hours to make his historic flight. There are 24 hours in a day. In days and hours, how long did his trip take?

Weatherman's Day
Born on February 5, 1744, John Jeffries was America's first weatherman.
1. Record the high and low temperatures for today.
2. Cut out a news article about the weather. Circle all the numbers in the article.
3. Write a math word problem about the weather.
4. Write a pretend weather story about a snowstorm that dropped four feet of snow on your town.

First American to Orbit the Earth
On February 20, 1962, John Glenn, Jr. became the first American and the third man to orbit the earth.
1. It is approximately 24,500 miles around the earth. How many miles did John Glenn travel?
2. Glenn circled the earth three times in less than five hours. How fast do you think he was going? How many minutes are there in five hours?

February Geography & Science

China: Lantern Festival

This traditional Chinese festival falls on the 15th day of the Chinese lunar calendar year's first month. This festival is characterized by lantern processions which mark the end of the Chinese New Year holiday season.

1. List the names of the seven continents. On which continent is China located?
2. Write about a traditional festival held in your own country.

International Friendship Week

International Friendship Week is held the last full week in February to promote international friendships.

1. Write the name of another country in which you would like to have a pen pal? Why does that country interest you?
2. Draw a symbol representing friendship that you could send to someone in another country.
3. Cut a one-inch-wide strip of paper. Decorate this paper to create a friendship bracelet that you could give to a friend. Tape it on your friend's wrist.

Grand Canyon National Park Established

This famous park was established on February 26, 1919.

1. Where is the Grand Canyon located? Find it on a map and write the name of the state.
2. Draw a picture of what you think the Grand Canyon would look like if you were in an airplane flying over it.

National Wild Bird Feeding Month

February is a time to encourage people to provide food, water and shelter for birds who have a tough time surviving in the wild during the winter months.

1. Make a list of winter birds.
2. Draw a picture of your favorite bird.
3. Make a list of the foods that birds like to eat.

Thomas Edison's Birthday

The famous scientist and inventor was born on February 11, 1847.

1. Make a list of some of the things that were invented by Thomas Edison.
2. This day is known as Inventor's Day. Write about the best invention ever.

Planet Pluto Discovered

On February 18, 1930, Pluto was discovered.

1. Pluto is the smallest planet. Write the names of the other eight planets.
2. Pluto got the first two letters of its name from the man who predicted the location of the ninth planet, Percival Lowell. Pluto was discovered 14 years after Lowell's death. Write what you would name a planet. Use your initials.

February Creative Writing Paper

March

March is the third month of the year. It was named after Mars, the mythological Roman God of War.

Bulletin Board Idea — Perfectly Pretty Poetry

Writing poetry can be a lot of fun for students. Even very young students are able to rhyme words in simple two- and three-word sentences.

Acrostic poems are also a form of poetry that young students can master. Here is an example:

M akes cakes.
A lways smiling.
R eads a lot.
Y ellow is her favorite color.

Learning Center Idea

The second Sunday in March is Plant a Flower Day. Place styrofoam cups or small clay pots by the window in your classroom. Add potting soil and flower seeds. The students will enjoy watching the flowers bloom!

The third week in March is National Wildlife Week. Place magazines full of wildlife pictures in the learning center. Let the students cut out pictures of various animals and then sort them according to which animals live in the oceans, in the forest, the jungle, deserts or the prairies.

March Language Arts

Music in Our Schools Month

March is a time to make the public aware of the importance of music education.
1. Draw a picture of your favorite instrument
2. Draw a musical note.
3. Write the name of your favorite kind of music.
4. Illustrate your favorite song.

National Poetry Month

This is a perfect time to let students enjoy reading and writing poems.
1. Write and illustrate your favorite poem.
2. Write a poem. Include "bike" and "hike" in it.
3. Design a cover for a poetry book.
4. Use each letter in your name to begin a sentence to create a poem about yourself.

Youth Art Month

March is a time to introduce students to all kinds of art.
1. Paint a picture.
2. Use crayons to draw the same picture you painted.
3. Make a collage of items that can be used in art.
4. Sketch a picture of yourself.

Newspapers In Education Week

The first week in February is a time when students can learn about the important information contained in newspapers.
1. Cut out an interesting article from a newspaper.
2. List the names of three sections of a newspaper.
3. Cut out a picture from a newspaper. Write a story to go with it.
4. Cut out a coupon from the newspaper.

Dr. Seuss' Birthday

This favorite children's author, Theodor Geisel, was born on March 2, 1904.
1. Write the title of your favorite Dr. Seuss book.
2. Draw a character from one of Dr. Seuss' books.
3. Write a story that could appear in a Dr. Seuss book. Include these words: dog, frog, hog, and log.
4. Design a cover and write a title for a new Dr. Seuss book.

March Social Studies

First Person in Space from Czechoslovakia

On March 2, 1978, Vladimir Remek became the first person in space from a country other than the United States or the U.S.S.R.
1. Draw a picture of yourself in space.
2. Write the name of a spaceship you would like to travel in. Draw it.
3. Finish this sentence: When we landed on the moon, ...

Girl Scout Week

This week is held to observe the founding of the Girl Scouts of the United States. It is the largest voluntary organization for girls and women in the world and was founded on March 12, 1912.
1. Draw a picture of something that Girl Scouts do.
2. Draw a picture of something yummy Girl Scouts sell.
3. Girl Scouts are five to seventeen years old. Describe one way in which you are a good citizen.

Uncle Sam's Birthday

Uncle Sam, a symbol of the United States first appeared decorated with stars and stripes on March 13, 1830.
1. Draw another symbol of the United States.
2. Draw a picture of something that could be a symbol for your class.
3. Write a letter to Uncle Sam about a concern you have about the United States.
4. Draw a 1990's version of Uncle Sam.

St. Patrick's Day

March 17 is the day when Bishop Patrick, the patron saint of Ireland, is honored.
1. Draw a symbol you often see on St. Patrick's Day.
2. Write the name of the color you are supposed to wear on St. Patrick's Day.
3. Draw a picture of you on St. Patrick's Day.
4. Finish this sentence: On St. Patrick's Day, I met the cutest little leprechaun and . . . .

Earth Day

March 20 or 21 is Earth Day, or Day of the Vernal Equinox. On this day, the sun crosses the equator (equinox), thus signalling the beginning of spring in the Northern Hemisphere and the beginning of autumn in the Southern Hemisphere.
1. Draw a picture of spring.
2. Draw a picture of you doing something in autumn.
3. Write the names of the other two seasons.
4. Write a rhyming poem beginning "I love the spring, ...

March Math

TV Turn-Off

This week-long event, held the second week in March, encourages people to turn off their televisions and do other activities.

1. Write how many hours of TV you watch each week.
2. Write how many hours of TV you would like to watch each week.
3. Make a collage of activities you enjoy.
4. Write a math word problem about TV.

Physical Education and Sports Week

The first week of March is dedicated to encouraging people to get out and get involved in athletic activity.

1. Find an article in a newspaper involving a sport. Circle the numbers in it.
2. Use the newspaper article and the numbers it contains to write a math word problem.
3. Draw a variety of sports balls. Write a math problem about them.
4. Find out your class' favorite sport.

Paper Money Issued

On March 10, 1862, the first paper money was issued in the United States.

1. Alexander Hamilton is on the $10 bill. Draw a picture of you on a bill. Write on the bill how much it is worth.
2. List what you can buy with $10.
3. Write a math word problem about money.
4. Draw a picture showing what you would do if you won a million dollars.

Planet Uranus Discovered

Uranus was discovered by Sir William Herschel on March 13, 1781.

1. Uranus is the seventh planet from the sun. Write the names of the other eight planets.
2. Uranus is thirty-one thousand, eight hundred miles in diameter. Write this number.
3. Write how many years ago Uranus was discovered.
4. Uranus is about 1 billion, seven hundred and eighty-three million, eight hundred thousand miles from the sun. Write out this numeral.

Daylight-Saving Time

Daylight-Saving Time first went into effect on March 31, 1918.

1. Daylight-Saving Time makes us lose one hour in the spring. Write what time it would be if Daylight-Saving Time took place at 1:30 a.m.
2. Write what time it is now.
3. Draw a clock. Draw hands on it to show your favorite time of day.
4. Write what time you go to bed.

March Geography & Science

Florida Became a State
Florida became the twenty-seventh state on March 3, 1845.
1. Draw an outline of Florida.
2. Draw an outline of your state.
3. Describe what activities you can do in Florida.

Amerigo Vespucci's Birthday
Born March 9, 1451, Vespucci was an explorer. North and South America were both named for him.
1. Write the name of a country in North America.
2. Draw the outline of South America.
3. Write the name of a country you would like to visit.
4. Draw the outline of the United States.

Eiffel Tower Anniversary
The Eiffel Tower was built for the Paris Exhibitions of 1889. Its anniversary is March 31.
1. Name the country where the Eiffel Tower is located.
2. Draw a picture of a famous United States landmark. Where is it located?
3. Write the name of a famous landmark in your state.
4. Design a new landmark for your city/town.

National Nutrition Month
March is dedicated to educating consumers about the importance of good nutrition.
1. Draw a healthy dinner.
2. Make a collage of healthy foods.
3. Explain why it is important to eat right.
4. Draw a picture showing what else you need to do to be healthy.

Alexander G. Bell's Birthday
On March 3, 1847, the man who invented the telephone was born.
1. Draw as many different kinds of telephones as you can.
2. Write your phone number and your best friend's phone number.
3. Write the phone numbers of people who can help you in an emergency.
4. Draw a picture of a phone you might be using in the year 2050.

National Wildlife Week
The third week in March is dedicated to the many forms of wildlife inhabiting our planet from the oceans to the tallest mountains.
1. Make a collage of jungle wildlife animals.
2. Finish this sentence: One day, while walking in the forest, I met a tiny little . . . .
3. Draw a picture of your favorite wild animal. Give it a name.

March Creative Writing Paper

April

April is the fourth month of the year. Its name comes from the Latin word *Aprilis,* which means to open.

Bulletin Board Idea — Very Nice Volunteers

The last week in April is National Volunteer Week. Talk about various kinds of volunteer opportunities: the hospital, libraries, nursing homes, school, etc. Do you have volunteers at your school? Who are these people? What do they do? Have the students create a bulletin board that thanks the people in your school building who are volunteers.

Learning Center Idea

National Week of the Ocean is in the middle of the month. Provide the students with various colors of construction paper, markers, crayons, scissors, and glue and let them create an ocean scene.

World Health Day is celebrated in the month of April. Provide the children with books that teach about good health and nutrition. Let the children make a list of things that we should do (or not do) to stay healthy: eat well, exercise, get plenty of rest, do not smoke, etc.

April Language Arts

National Humor Month

April is a time to celebrate the joy of laughter and its important role in our lives.
1. Laughter reduces stress. Describe one thing that stresses you out.
2. Draw a funny picture
3. Write and illustrate a "knock-knock" joke.
4. Draw a picture of you doing something funny.

April Fools' Day

The first day in April is a day when people can play tricks on others and not get in too much trouble for it.
1. Write about a trick you played on someone.
2. Draw a picture of someone playing a trick on you.
3. Write a poem. Include the words "fool" and "cool" in it.
4. Finish this sentence: One day, while I was playing a trick on my best friend . . . .

International Children's Book Day

April 2 is a day when children's literature is celebrated worldwide on this, the birthday of Hans Christian Andersen.
1. Write the name of your favorite author.
2. Draw your favorite character in a book.
3. Create a new cover for an old book.
4. Write the name of a book written by Hans Christian Andersen.

National Library Week

Held the second week in April, this event promotes the support and use of all kinds of libraries.
1. Write the name of your city/town's library.
2. Write the name of a person who works in a library.
3. Draw a sign you might see in a library.
4. Draw pictures of things you can borrow from a library.

National Bubble Gum Week

Held the fourth week in April, this event celebrates this chewy substance which can be blown into bubbles.
1. Draw a picture of you blowing a big bubble.
2. Finish this sentence: When I looked at the bubble I blew, I saw . . . .
3. Make a collage of other sweet treats.
4. Draw your favorite kind of bubble gum.

April Social Studies

Pony Express Began

On April 3, 1860, the Pony Express began when the first rider left St. Joseph, Missouri, and headed for Sacramento, California.

1. The Pony Express was a mail delivery service. Draw a picture of your mailbox.
2. Draw a picture of your mail carrier.
3. Write a letter to a friend.
4. Draw a picture of another means of communication.

Look-Alike Day

April 18 is a day to recognize people who look like someone famous.

1. Draw a picture of someone famous that you think you look like.
2. Cut out a picture of someone you would like to look like.
3. Finish this sentence: After I drank the magic potion, I looked in the mirror and saw . . . .
4. Write three words that rhyme with look.

Paul Revere's Ride

On April 18, 1775, Paul Revere made his famous ride from Boston, Massachusetts, to Concord, to warn the American patriots that the British were coming.

1. Write the name of the country the British were from.
2. Draw a picture of Paul Revere on his ride.
3. Pretend you rode with Paul Revere. Explain what you yelled to people on your ride.

National Pet ID Week

The third week in April is dedicated to encouraging people to properly identify their pets.

1. Write a pet ID for your pet, or for a pet you wish you had.
2. Draw a picture of your pet or one you would like to have, wearing an ID.
3. Explain why it is important for pets to have identification.

National Volunteer Week

Held the last week in April, this event honors those who help others in their community and encourages others to give of their time.

1. Write what you can do to help your community.
2. Make a collage of people volunteering in a community.
3. Write the name of a volunteer organization in your city.

April Math

Mathematics Education Month

April is a time when students, teacher, parents, and the community focus on the important role math plays in our lives.
1. Write three ways you use math every day.
2. Write a math word problem about parents.
3. Make a collage of numbers.
4. Write a poem about math. Include the words "math" and "bath" in it.

United States Mint Established

The first United States Mint was established on April 2, 1792 in Philadelphia, Pennsylvania.
1. Mint is a homograph. This means that it has several meanings. Draw a picture of another kind of mint.
2. Design a new bill. Write the amount it is worth on its front and back.
3. Write a math word problem involving money.
4. Write a story about how you earn your allowance.

Income Tax Pay-Day

By April 15, all Americans must pay taxes to the government.
1. Write three things tax money pays for.
2. Explain whether you think taxes are fair.
3. Draw a picture of how your parents feel after paying taxes.

Rubber Eraser Day

On April 15, 1770 an English chemist named the eraser when he discovered that a small piece of latex could erase pencil marks.
1. Design a new eraser. What does it look like? Besides erasing pencil marks, does it do anything else?
2. Explain why people like erasers.
3. Write a math word problem about erasers.
4. Draw some items you use during math class, besides an eraser.

National Coin Week

Coin collecting is promoted during the middle of April each year.
1. Draw three real coins. Label how much each is worth.
2. Draw six coins that would add up to 10¢.
3. Design a new coin. Designate what it is worth.
4. Explain why you think people do not use all coins, instead of bills.

April Geography & Science

North Pole Discovered

The North Pole was discovered by Robert E. Peary on April 6, 1909.
1. Draw a picture of the pole that is a symbol of the North Pole.
2. List what activities you could probably do at the North Pole.
3. Peary used a dog team and sled to get to the North Pole. Draw a picture of you leading a dog team.

National Read- A- Road Map Week

This week is a time when reading maps for fun is promoted.
1. Write the names of three important roads in your area.
2. Draw a map to show someone how to get from your house to school.
3. Draw a symbol often found on road maps. Define what it means.

National Week of the Ocean

In the middle of April, attention is focused on humanity's interdependence with the oceans of the world.
1. Write the name of the ocean along the east coast of the United States.
2. Draw a picture of and write the name of the ocean on the west coast of the United States.
3. Estimate how many miles it is from your house to the closest ocean.

Keep America Beautiful Month

April is dedicated to educating Americans about their responsibilities to prevent litter and to improve the environment.
1. Draw a picture showing what you can do to help the environment.
2. Draw a poster telling people not to litter.
3. Design a bumper sticker telling people to "Keep America Beautiful!"

National Science and Technology Week

The last week in April is a time when children and adults are made aware of science and technology.
1. Make a collage depicting state-of-the-art technology.
2. Draw a picture of a technological item you could not live without.
3. List five words you associate with science.

Arbor Day

The first observance of Arbor Day was April 10, 1872 in Nebraska. It is now celebrated on various dates around the world.
1. Arbor Day is a day set aside for planting trees. Write three reasons trees are important to the earth and people.
2. Draw a picture of three things made from trees.
3. Write a poem about a tree.

April Creative Writing Paper

May

May is the fifth month of the year. Many people believe that this month was named for *Maia,* the Roman Goddess of Spring.

Bulletin Board Idea — Look Where We've Been

The first week in May is National Postcard Week. Have the students create a picture postcard depicting a place they have been or some place that they would like to go. On the back they should write a note to a friend and tell something about their vacation.

Ask the children to bring in postcards that they might have at home. How big can you make a classroom postcard collection? Display on the bulletin board.

Learning Center Idea

Create a learning center that is designed for the children to locate materials that they may use in creating a Mother's Day card. Put a box of "odds 'n ends" in the learning center (sequins, craft jewels, ric-rac, ribbon, yarn, etc.).

The third week of May is National Transportation Week. Using boxes, paper plates, paints and other materials, have the students work in pairs to create a new form of transportation.

May Language Arts

Mother Goose Day
May 1 is dedicated to people's favorite Mother Goose nursery rhymes.
1. Write your favorite nursery rhyme.
2. Draw a character from your favorite nursery rhyme.
3. Draw a picture of Mother Goose.
4. Write a new nursery rhyme.

National Postcard Week
During the first week of May, people are encouraged to send postcards and to realize the fascinating information many of them contain.
1. Design a postcard with a picture of your city/town on it.
2. Write a postcard to a friend.
3. List the names of places you would like to get postcards from.
4. Draw a funny postcard picture.

National Teacher Day
The first Tuesday of the first full week in May is a day when teachers are honored for their hard work.
1. Design a "Teacher of the Year Award" to give to your favorite teacher.
2. Write a thank-you note to your favorite teacher.
3. Draw a present you would like to give your teacher.
4. Write a poem about your teacher.

Mother's Day
The second Sunday in May honors mothers everywhere.
1. Write three things you love about your mom.
2. Make a collage of pictures relating to your mom.
3. Make a Mother's Day card for your mom.
4. Write a thank-you note to your mom.

Memorial Day
Held the last Monday in May, Memorial Day honors those who have died in battle.
1. Write the name of a war the United States has been involved in.
2. Draw a United States flag.
3. Draw a picture of something many people do on Memorial Day.
4. Plan some fun events for your family to do on Memorial Day.

May Social Studies

May Day

Spring festivals and maypoles are commonly held on the first day in May.
1. Draw a maypole.
2. Write five words that rhyme with "May."
3. Draw a picture of a festival you have been to.
4. Write a poem about May.

National Tourism Week

The first week in May is dedicated to people who love to travel and explore new places. It is also a time when people are encouraged to do this more often.
1. Write about the best trip you ever took.
2. Draw a picture of a place you would like to visit.
3. Write the name of a place where someone you know lives, and with whom you like to visit.
4. Make a collage of places you would like to visit.

National Pet Week

The first full week in May is a time to promote public awareness of the importance of taking a pet to a veterinarian regularly.
1. Draw a pet you have or would like to have.
2. Make a collage of animals that would not make good pets.
3. Write a story about your favorite pet.
4. Finish this sentence: One day, my pet _____ looked at me and said . . . .

National Police Week

Established in 1963, this week is a time to honor the people who protect us every day.
1. Write about three things police officers do.
2. Draw a picture showing a police officer helping you.
3. Draw a picture of other people in the community who help you.
4. Write a thank-you note to the police officers in your town.

National Transportation Week

The week that includes the third Friday in May focuses attention on the many ways people have of traveling from one place to another.
1. Draw pictures of as many forms of transportation as you can.
2. Make a collage of the many forms of transportation.
3. Write a poem about your bike.
4. Draw a picture of your favorite way to travel.

May Math

National Bike Month
May celebrates bicycles as a great means of transportation and recreation.
1. "Bi" means two. Bicycles have two wheels. Write what "tri" means.
2. Write how many miles per hour you think you can ride on your bike.
3. Draw a picture of your bike.
4. Draw a speed limit sign for bicyclists.

Better Sleep Month
During May, good sleep is emphasized and Americans are encouraged to re-evaluate their bedtime habits.
1. Draw two clocks. Draw hands on them to show what time you go to bed and what time you get up.
2. Write how many hours you sleep each night.
3. Draw a clock with hands on it showing your favorite time of day.
4. Write one way you could sleep better.

National Family Week
The first Sunday and the first full week in May are celebrated as National Family Week.
1. Make a graph of the number of people each student in your class has in his/her family.
2. Add up the total number of family members your class has.
3. Write about an activity you could do this week with your family.
4. Draw a picture of the future family you hope to have when you grow up.

Gabriel Fahrenheit's Birthday
Born May 14, 1686, this German physicist developed the Fahrenheit temperature scale.
1. Write today's temperature in Fahrenheit degrees.
2. Write today's temperature in Celsius degrees.
3. Draw a thermometer. Write in the temperature you would like it to be today.
4. Draw a picture of you on your perfect weather day.

Kentucky Derby
On May 17, 1875, the first running of the Kentucky Derby took place.
1. The Kentucky Derby is a 11/4-mile race. Write the name of something that is about 11/4 miles from your house.
2. About 10,000 spectators watched the first Derby. Calculate how many more people this is than the number of students in your school.
3. The first winner won two thousand, eight hundred and fifty dollars. Write this numeral.
4. Draw a picture of you on a horse winning the Kentucky Derby.

May Geography & Science

Cinco de Mayo

On May 5 in Mexico, parades, festivals, dances, and speeches are held recognizing the Mexican victory over the French in 1862.
1. Draw a picture of a float in a parade you have seen.
2. Write the name of a dance you like to do.
3. *Cinco* means five in Spanish. Write another Spanish word.

Jamestown, Virginia Founded

On May 14, 1607, the first permanent English settlement was established at Jamestown, Virginia.
1. Write the names of five other states.
2. Write the name of a state that is located next to your state.
3. The Jamestown settlers were from England. England is located on the continent of Europe. What continent do you live on?

Amelia Earhart Crossed Atlantic Ocean

On May 20, 1932, Amelia Earhart became the first woman to fly solo across the Atlantic Ocean by completing her 2-day flight to Ireland.
1. Name a state that borders the Atlantic Ocean.
2. Is the Atlantic Ocean on the east or west coast of the United States?
3. Write the name of the ocean located on the other coast of the United States.

National Physical Fitness and Sports Month

May is a time for people and organizations to promote fitness activities and programs.
1. Write three reasons why exercise is good for you.
2. List your ten favorite activities or sports.
3. Make a collage of sports activities.

National Weather Observer's Day

May 4 is a day for all people who love to follow the weather.
1. Predict tomorrow's weather. Draw a picture of it.
2. Write the high and low temperatures for today.
3. Draw a picture of a tornado, hurricane, or snowstorm.

First American in Space

On May 5, 1961, Alan Shepard, Jr. became the first United States astronaut in space.
1. Draw a picture of you as an astronaut.
2. Design a spaceship. Describe where it will take you.
3. Finish this sentence: When Mr. Shepard and I took off into space, ...

May Creative Writing Paper

June

June is the sixth month of the year. Many people believe that its name came from the Latin word, *juniores,* meaning young men, or *Juno,* the Goddess of Marriage.

Bulletin Board Idea — Fantastic Flags

National Flag Week occurs during the week of June 14th. Attach a United States flag to the top left corner of the bulletin board. Explain its symbols and their meanings to the students. Then, provide the students with materials that they can use to create a new flag. This does not have to be a country flag. The children might wish to create a family flag, a school flag, or even a personal flag. Have the students explain their flags to the class and then display on the bulletin board.

Learning Center Idea

Father's Day is the third Sunday of the month. Provide the students with the necessary materials to make Father's Day cards for their dads, grandfathers, uncles, etc.

Summer begins on June 21 or 22. Write and illustrate a simple poem about summer.

June Language Arts

Adopt-A-Shelter-Cat-Month
During June, the adoption of homeless kittens and cats from local shelters is encouraged.
1. Draw a picture of a cat you have or would like to have. Write its name next to it.
2. Finish this sentence: One day, my kitten looked at me and told me . . . .
3. List three things cats need.
4. Find out how many students in your class own cats. Draw this many cats.

June Is Turkey Lovers' Month
June is a time when people are encouraged to eat turkey.
1. Draw a picture of a turkey using your hand as an outline.
2. Pretend you are a turkey. Describe how you like Thanksgiving.
3. Make a collage of foods you eat with turkey.
4. Write a poem about a turkey.

National Yo-Yo Day
Yo-yo contests, demonstrations, and promotions are held on this day during the middle of June.
1. Draw a picture of a super-duper yo-yo. Write what it can do.
2. Draw a picture of your favorite toy.
3. Finish this sentence: My yo-yo looked at me, told me he was dizzy and . . . .
4. Make a collage of toys.

National Little League Baseball Week
Held the week beginning with the second Monday in June, this event celebrates baseball for little ones.
1. Write the name of your favorite baseball player.
2. Cut out a news article about a baseball player.
3. Draw a picture of you playing baseball.
4. Describe the best baseball game you ever played or saw.

Father's Day
Held the third Sunday in June, this is a day to honor fathers everywhere.
1. Make a Father's Day card.
2. Write a poem about your dad.
3. Draw a picture of something you would like to give your dad.
4. Write a thank-you letter to your dad.

June Social Studies

National Patriots Month
Held June 6–July 4 each year, this event encourages people to wear red, white, and blue, to fly the United States flag, and to buy United States products.
1. Draw a United States flag.
2. Make a collage of items produced in the United States.
3. Draw a picture of you wearing red, white, and blue.
4. Write one way you are patriotic.

International Volunteers Week
The first seven days of June are dedicated to men and women all over the world who give their time to help others.
1. Describe one way you can help others.
2. Draw a picture of someone who volunteers to help you.
3. Draw a picture of you helping someone.
4. Write the name of a volunteer organization in your community.

National Flag Week
Held the week including June 14, this event encourages people to honor and display our country's flag.
1. Draw a picture of a place the United States flag is usually displayed.
2. Design a new flag for the United States.
3. Write three words describing the United States flag.
4. Write what you think of when you see the United States flag.

National Columnist's Day
The fourth Tuesday in June is dedicated to newspaper columnists.
1. Cut out an article from a newspaper written by a columnist.
2. Draw a picture for a newspaper. Give it a title.
3. Write the name of your city/town's newspaper.
4. Imagine that you are a newspaper columnist. Write a story for today's paper.

Helen Keller's Birthday
This American writer and worldwide advocate of help for the blind was born June 27, 1880.
1. Draw a picture of something that helps blind people.
2. Describe what you think it would be like to be blind.
3. Sight is one of your five senses. List the other four senses.
4. Draw a picture of the prettiest sight you have ever seen.

June Math

Donald Duck's Birthday
Donald Duck was "born" June 9, 1934.
1. Draw a picture of Donald Duck. Write how old he is.
2. Draw a birthday cake with candles on it for Donald.
3. Write a math word problem about Donald and his friends.
4. Calculate how much older Donald is than you.

National Baseball Hall of Fame Dedicated
One June 12, 1939, the National Baseball Hall of Fame and Museum was dedicated in Cooperstown, New York.
1. Cut out an article in the newspaper dealing with baseball. Circle the numbers in it.
2. Write a math word problem about a baseball game you played in or saw.
3. Draw baseballs. Write a math equation involving them.
4. Draw a picture of a baseball game. Include the score.

National Juggling Day
On June 17, many juggling clubs hold festivals to demonstrate, teach, and celebrate juggling.
1. Draw someone juggling. Write a math word problem involving the juggler and his/her balls.
2. Draw balls to represent how many a juggler normally uses.
3. Draw all kinds of balls. Write a math equation involving them.
4. Make a collage of things that could be juggled.

Mildred "Babe" Didrikson Zaharias' Birthday
Born June 26, 1914, Zaharias was an incredible athlete.
1. Zaharias won two gold medals in the Olympics. Write the date of the next Olympics.
2. In 1947, she won 17 straight golf championships. Draw a picture of you winning a golf tournament. Write your score.
3. Zaharias excelled in softball, swimming, figure skating, billiards, and football. Write a math word problem involving one of these sports.
4. Cut out a newspaper article about a wonderful athlete today. Circle the numbers in the article.

World War I Began and Ended
World War began on June 28, 1914 and ended June 28, 1919.
1. Write how long this war lasted.
2. Calculate how many years ago this war started.
3. Determine how many years ago this war ended.
4. Estimate how far Europe is from your city/town.

June Geography & Science

Chimborazo Day

On June 3, attention is focused on the shape of the earth by noting the fact that Mt. Chimborazo sticks out further into space than any other mountain.
1. Draw a picture of a huge mountain sticking out into space.
2. Pretend you are standing on the top of Mt. Chimborazo. Write what you can see.
3. A mountain is a geographical feature. Draw a picture of another one.
4. Explain where you can go in the United States to see mountains.

First Balloon Flight

On June 5, 1783, the first demonstration of a hot air balloon flight took place in France.
1. Draw a picture of a hot-air balloon you would like to travel in.
2. Write the name of a country you would like to travel to in a hot-air balloon.
3. Write a word in French
4. Draw a picture of something you might see in France.

Summer Begins

Summer begins June 21 or 22 in the Northern Hemisphere.
1. Write in which hemisphere you are located.
2. Draw a picture of the season that is beginning in the Southern Hemisphere.
3. Draw a picture of you doing something fun in the summer.

June Dairy Month

June salutes American dairy producers.
1. Make a collage of dairy products.
2. Explain why dairy products are good for you.
3. Draw a picture of other foods that are good for you.
4. Pretend you are a dairy cow. What would you do today?

Fireworks Safety Month

During June, parents and children are warned of the dangers of playing with fireworks.
1. Draw a picture of fireworks.
2. Fireworks are an explosive. Draw a picture of another kind of explosive.
3. Describe how fireworks can be dangerous.

First American Woman in Space

On June 18, 1983, Dr. Sally Ride became the first American woman in space.
1. Draw a space shuttle you would like to travel in.
2. Describe where in space you would like to go and why.
3. Finish this sentence: When we got out of the space shuttle, we saw . . . .
4. Draw a picture of you being the first to do something in space.

June Creative Writing Paper

July

July is the seventh month of the year. It was once called *Julius,* named after Julius Caesar.

Bulletin Board Idea — Boring? No Way!

July is Anti-Boredom Month. Have the students make a huge collage of pictures they have cut out, or have drawn, that depict activities that one can do to avoid becoming bored.

The first zoo opened in Philadelphia in July, 1874. Assign various animals to small groups of students. The children can locate pictures of their assigned animals and then create them from construction paper. Cover the background of the bulletin board in white construction paper. Have the students turn this background into a mural of natural environments for their constructed animals to live in. Most zoos no longer have cages, so try to provide humane, natural environments.

Learning Center Idea

July is National Ice Cream Month. Let the students have the fun of making their own ice cream. Here is a simple recipe that can be made in a learning center.

You will need: 1 cup egg substitute* (amount equivalent to 4 eggs), 13/4 cups sugar, 21/2 tsp. vanilla, 1 pint half & half cream, 1 pint whipping cream, 1/2 gallon 2% low fat or whole milk, 2 - 3.9 oz. boxes instant dark chocolate pudding (or vanilla pudding for vanilla ice cream).

What you do: Mix together the sugar, egg substitute, half & half cream, vanilla, and whipping cream in a large bowl. Add instant pudding to mixture and stir. Slowly add the milk and stir the mixture until the pudding is dissolved. Pour the mixture into the ice cream maker and follow manufacturer's instructions.

* The egg substitute or real egg product can be found in the dairy section of the grocery store. This product has a pasteurized egg white base.

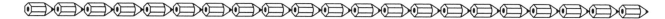

July Language Arts

National Baked Bean Month
July is a time people can pay tribute to one of America's most nutritious foods—baked beans.
1. Draw all kinds of foods usually eaten with baked beans.
2. Draw a picture of a time when people usually eat baked beans.
3. Write the names of three other kinds of beans.
4. Write a poem about a mean green bean named Dean.

National Hot Dog Month
July is a time to celebrate the sixteen billion hot dogs sold in the United States each year.
1. Draw a hot dog you would like to eat.
2. Make a collage of other barbecue foods.
3. Write a recipe involving hot dogs.
4. Draw a picture of an event at which hot dogs are sold.

National July Belongs to Blueberries Month
People are made aware that July is the peak month for fresh blueberries.
1. Write the names of three other kinds of berries.
2. Draw a field of blueberries.
3. Draw a picture of a food containing blueberries.
4. Write a recipe calling for blueberries.

Dog Days
July 3–August 15, the hottest days of the year in the Northern Hemisphere, are nicknamed Dog Days.
1. Draw a thermometer showing how hot it usually gets in your area during Dog Days.
2. Draw a picture of the season people in the Southern Hemisphere (opposite of ours) experience when we have summer.
3. Draw a picture of a dog to represent these days.
4. Describe what you think "cat days" are.

P.T. Barnum's Birthday
Born July 5, 1810, P.T. Barnum helped formed the most famous circus in history, the Ringling Brothers and Barnum & Bailey Circus.
1. Draw a picture of your favorite circus performance.
2. Finish this sentence: The best circus I ever went to . . .
3. Draw a picture of a clown.
4. Make a collage of foods you might eat at a circus.

July Social Studies

Anti-Boredom Month

July is dedicated to encouraging people to overcome boredom.
1. Draw a picture of something you can do when you are bored.
2. Bored and board are homophones. Write another one.
3. Write about one thing that bores you.

First Adhesive United StatesPostage Stamp Issued

The first adhesive United States postage stamps were issued by the United States Postal Service on July 1, 1847.
1. Write how much a postage stamp costs today.
2. Write the definition of "adhesive."
3. Design a new United States postage stamp.
4. Draw an envelope. Include the address of a friend and your return address.

Independence Day

The adoption of the Declaration of Independence on July 4, 1776, is celebrated by the United States every July 4.
1. Write about a special July 4th you have celebrated.
2. Draw a picture of a 4th of July celebration.
3. Write the name of another United States holiday.
4. Draw foods many people eat at July 4th celebrations.

"America The Beautiful" Published

The poem "America the Beautiful" was written by Katherine Lee Bates. It was first published July 4, 1895.
1. Copy your favorite poem. Illustrate it.
2. Draw a picture of something that makes America beautiful.
3. Write about something in your town that is beautiful.
4. Beautiful is a three-syllable word. Write three more three-syllable words that relate to America.

Freedom Week

July 4–10 is a time dedicated to informing people worldwide about freedom and liberty.
1. Describe three freedoms you enjoy.
2. Draw a picture of something you are free to do.
3. Write a poem about freedom.
4. Finish this sentence: I am glad I am free because . . . .

July Math

National Tennis Month
July is a perfect time for everyone to play tennis.
1. Write the order of points awarded in a game of tennis.
2. Cut out an article about a tennis player. Circle the numbers.
3. Write a math word problem involving tennis.
4. Draw four different types of balls in order, going from largest to smallest.

First United States Bank Opened
The first United States bank opened in New York on July 3, 1819.
1. Two thousand, eight hundred and seven dollars were deposited the first day. Write this numeral.
2. Do you have more or less than this amount?
3. Cut out an article in the newspaper dealing with money.
4. Make a collage of things you would do or buy with this amount of money.

Air conditioning Appreciation Days
July 3 to August 15, the hottest time of the year, is a great time for people to appreciate air conditioning.
1. Find out what your school's air conditioning bill is for this month.
2. Estimate what temperature you think it is in your school.
3. Draw a thermometer to show the temperature outside.
4. Write a math word problem about temperature.

Day of the Five Billion
On July 11, 1987, a baby boy was pronounced the five billionth inhabitant of Earth.
1. Write the number 5 billion.
2. Write the population of your city/town.
3. Draw as many people as you can on one piece of paper. Write how many people you drew on the back of the paper.
4. Write a math word problem involving a large number of people.

Terry Fox Day
Born July 28, 1958, Terry Fox planned a "Marathon of Hope" to raise money for cancer. This was a 5,200 mile run across Canada.
1. Fox had cancer and had his right leg removed at age 18 because of it. Determine the year he turned 18.
2. Fox only ran 3,328 miles of his marathon because of his cancer. Calculate how many miles he was not able to run.
3. Fox raised $24 million for cancer research. Write this number.
4. Fox started running April 12, 1980, and stopped September 1, 1980. How many months was he running?

July Geography & Science

National Recreation and Parks Month

July is a great time for all people to enjoy a variety of leisure activities.
1. Write the name of a park near your house where people can go to participate in activities.
2. Draw a park in your state. Write its name.
3. Write the name of a state you would like to visit.
4. Draw a picture of yourself doing your favorite activity.

First Zoo Established

On July 1, 1874, the first United States zoo opened in Philadelphia.
1. Write the name of the zoo nearest to your home.
2. Draw a zoo animal. Write what kind of climate it normally lives in.
3. Design a T-shirt a zoo could sell.
4. Draw a zoo animal that lives in water. In which body of water does it usually live?

Respect Canada Day

On July 15, people should try to show our Canadian friends that we know that they are not just a strange northern province of America.
1. Draw an outline of Canada.
3. Besides English, write what other language many Canadians speak.
4. Write a letter to someone in Canada. Ask three questions in your letter.

National Ice Cream Month

July is a great time for everyone to enjoy America's favorite dessert.
1. Ice cream is a dairy product. Draw three other dairy products.
2. Besides dairy products, write the names of other foods that are good for you.
3. Cut out pictures of foods that will make a healthy meal.
4. Draw a big ice cream cone you would like to eat.

Typewriter Invented

William Burt had the first American patent for a typewriter. It was invented sometime in July, 1829.
1. Draw another type of invention similar to the typewriter.
2. Draw a picture of an incredible invention you created.
3. Make a collage of wonderful inventions.
4. Draw the letter keys of a typewriter. Write in the correct letters.

Space Week

This week is held to expand public support for the United States Space program.
1. Design a poster for this week.
2. Write ten words relating to "space.".
3. Cut out an article from a newspaper dealing with our space program.

July Creative Writing Paper

August

August is the eighth month of the year. It was named after Emperor Augustus.

Bulletin Board Idea — Fantastic Friends

The first Sunday in August is Friendship Day. Cover the bulletin board with yellow paper. Create a caption at the top of the bulletin board that says. "Friends are...." Have each of the students write one word on a piece of paper that describes what a friend should be. Have the students create an illustration to accompany their "friend" words.

Learning Center Idea

The first Sunday in August is American Family Day. Provide the students with show boxes and many odds and ends that they can use to create a diorama depicting their families.

Dream Day is August 28. Provide the students with cotton batting that they can use as cloud material. Glue the cloud to a piece of construction paper. On an index card, have the children write about a dream they have experienced. Glue the cards onto the clouds.

August Language Arts

International Clown Week

Every August 1–7 is dedicated to the charitable activities of clowns and the wholesome entertainment provided around the world.
1. Draw a picture of a happy clown. Write its name next to it.
2. List three things clowns do.
3. Draw a picture of a place you find a clown.
4. Write a poem about clowns.

Friendship Day

The first Sunday in August is a day for people to acknowledge old friends and celebrate new ones.
1. Make a card for a good friend.
2. Write three things a friend does.
3. Draw a picture of you and your best friend.
4. Finish this sentence: A good friend is someone who . . . .

American Family Day

The first Sunday in August is designated to celebrate the family.
1. Draw a picture of your family.
2. Finish this sentence: My family is the greatest because . . . .
3. Cut out pictures of things your family likes to do.
4. Plan something your family could do on this day.

Middle Children's Day

This day is held during the middle of August and salutes the middle child, who was always told he/she was too young or too old.
1. Draw a picture of you as a middle child. If you do not have an older and younger brother/sister, draw yourself one of each.
2. Draw a picture of something you are too young to do.
3. List three things you are too old to do.
4. Write about what you think is the perfect age, when you can do whatever you want.

International Lefthanders Day

August 13 is a day when the needs and frustrations of lefthanders are recognized.
1. Draw a picture using your "opposite" hand.
2. Write your name with your "opposite" hand.
3. Carefully cut out pictures using your "opposite" hand.
4. Finish this sentence: I am glad I use the hand I do because . . . .

August Social Studies

Francis Scott Key's Birthday
Born August 1, 1779, Francis Scott Key wrote our country's national anthem.
1. Write the name of our national anthem.
2. Draw a picture of the star-spangled banner.
3. Make a list of occasions when you might sing the National Anthem.
4. Write the name of your favorite song.

Louis Armstrong's Birthday
This famous jazz musician was born August 4, 1901.
1. Draw a picture of your favorite musical instrument.
2. Describe your favorite kind of music is.
3. Make a list of your favorite songs.
4. Draw some musical notes.

Coast Guard Day
The United States Coast Guard was founded on August 4, 1790.
1. Draw a picture of the vehicles the Coast Guard uses.
2. The Coast Guard protects life and property at sea. Write the name of an ocean they could work in.
3. The Coast Guard tests life vests to make sure they are safe. Draw a picture of yourself in your life vest.
4. Write a thank you letter to the Coast Guard.

National Relaxation Day
August 15 is a time when everyone should totally relax.
1. Draw a picture of you relaxing.
2. Make a collage of pictures depicting things people can do to relax.
3. Explain what happens to people if they do not relax.
4. Draw a poster for this day.

Dream Day
Three events are remembered on August 28, one being the March on Washington (1963) led by Martin Luther King, Jr. He delivered his famous "I Have a Dream" speech on this day.
1. King dreamt of peace and equality for all. Write about a dream you have for our world.
2. Draw a picture of a funny dream you had.
3. Cut out an article dealing with a famous African-American.
4. King believed in nonviolence. How do you solve problems?

August Math

Foot Health Month

August is dedicated to educating people about the importance of taking care of their feet.

1. What size shoe do you wear? Identify what size it would be if it were five sizes larger.
2. Trace around your shoe. Decorate it.
3. Measure how many inches long your foot is.
4. Using your feet to measure, compute the distance from your desk to some object of your choice.

Maria Mitchell's Birthday

Born August 1, 1818, she became the first female professional astronomer.

1. Mitchell was very good in math. Write a math word problem about yourself.
2. Draw something an astronomer looks for in the sky.
3. Draw a constellation. Name it.
4. Write how old Mitchell would be today if she were still alive.

National Mustard Day

Every August 5 is dedicated to mustard lovers everywhere.

1. Draw pictures of foods you like mustard on.
2. Find out how many students in your class like mustard better than ketchup.
3. Write a math word problem involving mustard.
4. Draw a bottle of mustard. Write its price on it.

Halfway Point of Summer

August 7 or 8 is the halfway point of summer.

1. How much summer is left on this day?
2. Write the month in which summer ends.
3. Draw a picture of you doing something fun during the summer.
4. Write a math word problem about summer.

Krakatoa Erupted

On August 26, 1883, the volcanic island of Krakatoa erupted.

1. The eruption killed thirty-six thousand people. Write this numeral.
2. Tidal waves 120 feet high were created. Write how many feet taller these were than you are now.
3. The explosion was heard 3,000 miles away. Write the name of a place you think is this far from your house.
4. Calculate how many years ago Krakatoa erupted.

August Geography & Science

United States Customs Established

On August 1, 1789, the first United States Customs officers began their job of collecting revenue and enforcing the Tariff Act of July 4, 1789.

1. The United States Custom Service sets and collects taxes on imported goods. Draw a picture of something you have that came from another country.
2. Cut out three pictures of things that are made in the United States.
3. The Customs Service regulates goods, people, and vehicles entering or leaving the United States. List the countries you would like to visit.

United States War Department Established

On August 7, 1789, Congress established the War Department.

1. Write the name of a war the United States has been involved in.
2. Cut out a news article dealing with war. Circle the countries' names in it.
3. Finish this sentence: I do not think there will ever be a war in the United States because . . . .

Hawaii Became 50th State

Hawaii became the 50th state on August 21, 1959.

1. Hawaii is known as the "Aloha State." Write your state's nickname.
2. Islands make up Hawaii. Draw an island you would like to visit.
3. Hawaii has a very mild climate. Draw five things you would take on a trip to Hawaii.
4. Pretending you are in Hawaii, write a postcard to a friend.

National Water Quality Month

August is a time when people are encouraged to realize the importance of water as a precious resource.

1. Write three things you can do to conserve water.
2. Draw a picture of three places you can find water.
3. List the three things that can pollute water.

First Oil Well Drilled

On August 27, 1859, W.A."Uncle Billy" Smith is given credit for drilling the first oil well in the United States.

1. Write three things we use oil for.
2. What kind of oil do many people like to use when they are cooking?
3. This first oil well was drilled in Pennsylvania. Draw a picture of an oil well.

National Aviation Day

This day is held on Orville Wright's birthday (August 19). It honors the man who piloted the first self-powered flight in history.

1. Design a poster for this day.
2. Write the names of other vehicles people use for travel.
3. Make a paper airplane. See how far it can go.

August Creative Writing Paper

US COAST GUARD

Happy Daughter's Day

I Have a Dream.

Journal Writing Ideas

September _____

_____

_____

_____

_____

_____

October _____

_____

_____

_____

_____

_____

November _____

_____

_____

_____

_____

_____

Journal Writing Ideas

December _____

_____

_____

_____

_____

_____

January _____

_____

_____

_____

_____

_____

February _____

_____

_____

_____

_____

_____

Journal Writing Ideas

March _____

_____

_____

_____

_____

_____

_____

April _____

_____

_____

_____

_____

_____

_____

May _____

_____

_____

_____

_____

_____

_____

Journal Writing Ideas

June _____

_____

_____

_____

_____

_____

July _____

_____

_____

_____

_____

_____

_____

August _____

_____

_____

_____

_____

_____